PARENTING RESET:

A Practical Guide on Infusing Love and Gratitude into your Parenting Journey

◇◇◇◇◇◇◇◇

DR. TERENCE HOUSTON

&

DR. EARDIE HOUSTON

COPYRIGHT © 2018 EARDIE HOUSTON

All rights reserved.

No part of the material protected by this copyright may be reproduced or utilized in any form, electronic or mechanical, including photocopying, recording, or any information storage and retrieval system, without written persmission from the copyright owner.

ISBN: 978-1-947574-04-5

To David, Joshua, and Christian

*You are our greatest blessings and our best teachers.
We love you more than you'll ever know.*

Contents

Faith • 1

Acceptance/Love • 15

Prioritizing the Marriage • 29

Protection/Boundaries/Safety • 39

Structure/Discipline • 51

Fun • 61

Acknowledgements

Introduction

This guide intends to capture some of our best practices as parents. This is not to suggest that our parenting philosophies are perfect, but we firmly believe that we can learn from one another as parents. It is our desire to share with others the practices that we do well, to offer tools to other parents who may not have considered some of these strategies.

People within our sphere of influence often ask us for parenting advice. Many have noticed that our parenting style is very intentional. Some ask where our ideas and parenting concepts come from. That's a tough question to answer. Some of it comes from our upbringing. We came from two very different backgrounds. One, from a solid, traditional, healthy environment. The other, from a broken home. We've brought together experiences from our families of origin and our ideas of what to do and what not to do. Ultimately, we realized that we really have to trust God and be intentional about seeking His wisdom concerning how to raise our children. We pray a lot. We read a lot. And importantly, we pay attention to our children. We listen to them, the spoken and the unspoken. We make mistakes, learn from them, and adjust. We find things that work well and duplicate those wins as much as we can. And those wins are what we've captured in this resource.

Our parenting pillars include:

1. Faith
2. Acceptance / Love
3. Prioritizing the Marriage
4. Safety
5. Structure
6. Fun

Faith
Chapter 1

We're so thankful that even at such a young age, our children are beginning to show evidence that they are internalizing what we are teaching them about our faith. We believe that faith is the foundational cornerstone that will enable them to navigate life in a world that is so unpredictale. There are several practices that we have, and continue to employ to teach, and then reinforce the teachings.

Consistent Teaching

The two keys to this practice for children (and probably adults, too) are both the consistency and the small doses of information. It's been well demonstrated over the years that small, consistent changes over time can reap an abundance of results, positive or negative, depending on what is sown.

BRIEF DEVOTIONS (2-3 MINUTES)

By brief, we do mean brief! In the mornings, we often wake our children up (on the mornings that they haven't gotten up before us!) with a simple song with one refrain, sang over and over. "Good morning, God! This is your day! I am your child! Show me your way!" Once we say our good mornings, we say, "Did you thank God for another day?" To which they either reply "Yes" or "Thank you, God, for another day." Very simple.

On the way to school, we commonly ask questions like, "How are you going to be a light today?" And we each say a short prayer before getting out of the car in the morning. Just as it is important for us as adults to center ourselves and prepare for the day, it is equally as important for children to start their days off with an intentional focus on honoring God.

Consistent Bedtime Routine (Bible story, Song, Prayer)

Almost all families have a bedtime routine. We've found that this time is an excellent opportunity to end the day as we started, with an intentional focus on God. For us, that routine has been a Bible story (read from a children's story bible), followed by a song, and then prayers by each member of the family. (Yes, even the toddler!) We're constantly surprised by how much knowledge they have of the Bible. And it's likely that much of it can be attributed to the daily readings. Even in small doses, over time, they absorb so much. The songs are fun, too! We do a lot of the childhood favorites, like "Jesus Loves Me" and "He's Got the Whole World," etc.

With Terence having grown up in the A.M.E. church, we've adopted the practice of teaching our children old hymns, as well. They really get a kick out of learning songs that Daddy and Mommy learned as children. That sometimes sparks other meaningful dialogue where they invite us to share information with them, which they relish! We have developed in our children the practice of prayer, even before they understood what it was, and while they're still learning the importance of it.

Daily prayer time puts the foundation in place, and it also creates an opportunity for us to come together once more as a family at the end of the day, and express gratitude, concerns, fears, and successes. This has been very meaningful for the children, and for us.

Optimize Teachable Moments

Take advantage of opportunities to apply learnings from Bible teaching, and other character and faith lessons. As parents, we're constantly trying to take advantage of moments to reinforce things they are learning, whether colors, phonics principles, telling time, etc. Well, we believe that it's also important to do that regarding lessons they are learning about our faith. It's very common in our home to summon the story of David and Goliath when a real-life situation calls for faith and courage, or to bring up Jonah when faced with a situation of disobedience. We help them connect the dots and see that these stories aren't just for our entertainment, but stories for us to learn from. And from that, we're seeing them begin to connect the dots on their own in certain situations.

Sunday School / BSF

It truly does take a village. We're so fortunate to be in a church culture that places so much emphasis on equipping children, as much as adults. Many churches now have a structured children's program that supports parents in the desire to pour into children in ways that will "Train them up in the way they should go." In addition to our local church, we have also been fortunate to participate in a program called Bible Study Fellowship (BSF).

BSF is an in-depth, interdenominational Bible study that helps people know God and equips them to serve the Church throughout the world effectively. We initially began attending BSF out of our desire to learn more about God's Word, and then as an added bonus, we found out about their Children's Program. "Great! There's childcare," we thought to ourselves. But wow, it is more than just childcare. Their children's program is one in which children of all ages are taught the Word of God in ways that they are able to digest it at their level. We have already witnessed in our children the amazing growth that they've experienced in this program.

Call to Action:

Create your own 15-minute end of day routine. Ex. Moments of gratitude from the day, prayer, what to work on tomorrow.

Bonus Action

Find your nearest BSF and explore their program. It will be such a blessing, for your children, and for you!

www.bsfinternational.org

Modeling Behaviors Consistently for Them

Many of us can remember adults saying some variation of the phrase "Do as I say, not as I do." Well, we think many of us can agree that even though we likely complied, that still isn't the most effective way to instruct and direct our children. After all, it's commonly stated that with children, "More is caught, than taught." They're always watching us and picking up their behavior cues from us. We've often commented that our kids are always paying attention, especially when we don't want them to. They notice when we're not obeying the speed limit, and they notice when we've spoken a cross word to one another. It's so important that we are aware that we're always teaching them something with our behavior, whether we intend to, or not.

DEMONSTRATE INTEGRITY IN RELATIONSHIPS

This means inside and outside of the home. Is your marriage grace-filled? Are your friendships genuine? Children pick up on the energy of anger, insincerity, maliciousness, unforgiveness... Do they witness you treat your spouse with kindness? Do they hear you gossip about your "friends?" We have to be aware that we are teaching them to be a certain kind of man/woman, husband/wife, father/mother, friend. What if they treated their spouse like you treat yours? Or better yet, what if their spouse treated them like you treat yours? This is something to ponder since we have a great deal of influence over what they will grow to see as "normal" and "acceptable" behavior. And the cornerstone of that is what they see in us.

REGULAR PRAYER AND BIBLE STUDY/CHURCH ATTENDANCE

It's one thing to have prayer and Bible study for the sake of teaching them to do it, but we're talking about us, as parents, actually recognizing the need to have these behaviors as a part of our DNA. Praying and reading the Word when they're not around to see it. Actually adopting these practices for our own lives. Then, we are not only modeling it for their sake but importantly, giving ourselves the opportunity to learn and grow in the Word. They'll benefit not only from the example but also from the fruits of your spirit.

Generosity to Others
(Allowing Them to Be a Part of It)

Are you generous to others in word and deed? How do they see you respond to requests for your time, energy, or resources? Often as parents, we encourage our children to share with others. But do they see that behavior in us? Take them along on a visit to see a sick or elderly person. Clue them in on a service project that you are working on. Allow them to be a part of your routine clothes/toys/shoes charity drive. Not only for their giveaways, but for yours, as well. Demonstrate genuine care and concern for others.

Regularly Discussing Gratitude

Not just in prayer, but in conversation. One of the conversations we have in frequent, small doses is one of gratitude. Not in a forced interrogation that requires them to list everything that they're grateful for, but rather in the natural course of everyday conversation. It's very common for us to verbally express gratitude over things like getting in the short line at the grocery store or timing our approach so that we drive up just as someone is leaving a great parking space. Allow your children to hear that. It sends the message that gratitude is appropriate at all points of the day, not just specific prayer times. Besides, doesn't it feel good to celebrate something? It's so much more satisfying than complaining!

Call to Action:

Start by developing the healthy habit of daily time with God (for yourself). They'll see it; both, see you doing it and see the changes in you.

Moving Beyond the Templates and Encouraging Them to Grow in Their Own Faith Journey

We believe what we believe. That's obvious. Therefore, we teach our children about the things that we believe about our faith. We are teaching them things we believe to be true. With that said, however, we also know that at some point in life (or many points along the way), they will choose what they believe. Therefore, we recognize the importance of giving them all the knowledge and practice while they are young, knowing that as they grow, they must choose to accept or reject these teachings into their hearts. It's common for believers (regardless of faith belief) to regurgitate what they're told/taught, without ever really absorbing the truth as their own. That's not what we want for our children.

Lord's Prayer vs Individual Prayers

It's amazing to see the evolution of their prayers in these early years. They've already moved beyond reciting prayers that have been taught, to actually expressing their own thoughts, questions, gratitude, and concerns to God. Don't get me wrong; we thought it was very important to teach them to learn, memorize, and recite "The Lord's Prayer," which we have done and continue to reinforce. In addition to that, though, we encourage them to talk to God as they talk to one of us. We think it's important for them to share their own heart with God.

"Random" Questions to Prompt Thought and Discussion about Lessons Learned at Home, Church, or BSF

Not just your typical "What did you learn in Sunday School today?" This is more so the approach that allows them to begin to think for themselves of how to apply the things they are learning. As an example, during a recent BSF year, we were studying the book of (John's Letter of) Revelation. Naturally, we were made aware each week of their lesson topics and key messages for them to learn. One day, one of our children came into the room as Mommy was journaling and asked what she was doing. Instead of Mommy telling him that she was journaling, which he wouldn't have understood anyway, she told him that she was "writing a letter to God" to which he replied, "Like John?" As you can imagine, this led to quite the interesting conversation during which he told Mommy his thoughts on writing letters to God. Mommy mostly let him talk, and occasionally peppered him with questions just to see how much he understood about the subject. This is a very helpful practice, as it helps us as parents know more about what areas we should spend more effort teaching about and also ways that we can pray for them regarding understanding and direction.

Helping Them "Connect the Dots" in Relationships with School Friends and Each Other

Help your child make the shift from awareness/knowledge to implementation. One example that comes to mind is a time during preschool when both of our sons would come home repeatedly telling us about another child at school who, according to them, disobeyed the teachers and didn't treat the other children (including them) with kindness. After a few weeks of concerning reports, we met with the school directors and expressed concerns about our children being exposed to a negative environment. After a short period, however, we realized that complaining wasn't the best approach to take. Instead, we felt led to reach out to the other family, and in doing so, we learned about certain circumstances within their family that were leading to some of the child's behavior. After communicating with the other mom, and a few playdates, not only did we stop hearing bad reports, but the child became one of David and Joshua's best friends.

There was a lesson in this for them, and for us. We teach them about forgiveness and living peacefully with others. But we realize that it's not enough to talk about it. We have to teach them how to apply these lessons. In fact, we know that it's good for us, too, for we haven't fully mastered any of this either. So together as a family, we're growing in our ability to live out our faith, not just in theory, but in action.

Not Always Answering the Questions for Them, but Rather Using Questions as an Opportunity to Engage in Discussion

"Well, what do you think?" Parenting is often the land of a thousand questions. And that grows exponentially when more than one child is in the home. As our kids get older, we have begun to resist the urge to answer all of their many questions outright. Instead, we see their questions as opportunities to engage in discussion. Sometimes, when a question is asked about God, rather than providing an answer, we'll ask, "Well, what do you think?" This leads to them summoning their own learnings and experiences to draw their own conclusion. As they grow, and this practice continues, we hope that it leads to them having their own clarity regarding what they believe.

Call to Action:

Tonight/today, rather than saying, "God is great, God is good..." or "Now I lay me down to sleep...," start the prayer time by saying, "God can hear us? What do you want to say to Him?"

Prayer

∞

Praying for them, with them, and encouraging them to pray for others. Prayer is one of the most powerful tools we have as Christians. Unfortunately, though, it's often significantly under-utilized. In our opinion, one of the most awesome aspects of prayer is that, when used effectively, it leads to peace. There's such peace in knowing that we have access to the Creator, the One who is in complete control. Just the act of prayer itself serves as a reminder to us that we have the greatest Supporter and Champion we could ever imagine.

Asking God for Wisdom Regarding How to "Train Them Up"

As parents, one of the most important things we can do for our children is to pray for them. Some of us are guilty of only praying in times of crisis; a major illness or accident, a child choosing the wrong friends and/or the wrong path. But it is important that we make a habit of praying for them outside of those times of deep concern. Pray for the man/woman that your child is to become. We pray for their health, their safety, their intellectual and social development. We also pray and ask God to give us wisdom and direction concerning how to nurture their gifts and concerning various specific situations we encounter with them.

Nurturing their gifts – we recognize that God has a specific design for each of our lives. Now, we don't pretend to know exactly what God has planned for each of our children (nor do we know all that He has planned for us!), but we do notice certain strengths and natural abilities that they have. We notice certain personality traits that add to their uniqueness. We ask God to give us wisdom regarding how we should encourage certain behaviors in them and which behaviors we should redirect. Specific situations – frequently we seek wisdom regarding the educational decisions we are making for them. We pray for guidance regarding how to discipline them or how to correct certain behavioral tendencies. There's always a reason to pray for our children. The time spent praying for them is never wasted.

Praying With Them

We covered earlier, the value of praying with our children. It gives us the opportunity to hear their hearts and we can't emphasize the importance of this practice enough. We just can't emphasize this enough. Not only is it a time to model communication with God in prayer, but it is very important to hear what's on their minds. Prayer time with them gives us insight into their days. We hear from their mouths what is in their hearts. With that insight, we're informed of areas that we need to increase our teaching or issues that we need to help them work through. Above all, we listen for things that the two of us can continue to pray about, long after they've gone to sleep.

Encouraging Them to Pray For Others

We tell them about challenges/concerns that family members have in a way that they can (somewhat) understand. With that, they have begun the practice of praying for the concerns of others. This can be comical at times, as we hold in our laughter while listening to them pray for their interpretations of the issues that we've shared with them. And even more comical when they pray for things like, "Dear God, please help my sister stop talking while I'm praying because she's being rude." Overall, we believe that the practice of praying for the concerns of others will help them become more compassionate and God-honoring as they show love and concern for others.

Celebrate With Them When Prayers Are Answered

And talk about it when it seems like they aren't. We often "call out" answered prayers to our kids because we recognize that it's easy to overlook when our prayers are answered. As we flow with the pace of life, it's easy to forget that we even prayed those prayers to begin with. This point is useful for the children and the adults.

In recent years, Eardie has practiced the discipline of keeping a prayer journal. A record, of sorts, of prayers prayed and answered. There's something special about being able to look back and acknowledge the prayers that have been answered. It strengthens one's faith while waiting for the ones that haven't been answered. Also, we think it's important to have an awareness of answered prayers because it increases our level of gratitude. Likewise, reminding the kids of their answered prayers increases their gratitude. We hope to set the stage for them to develop these muscles and flex them on their own as they grow older.

Resource – "Childbirth Promises," Circle Maker for Kids.

Not Shielding Them from Other Belief Systems

Help them understand the value of diversity of thought and beliefs and create opportunity for them to stand for what they're learning to believe in even when challenged.

ENGAGE IN CONVERSATIONS ABOUT DIFFERENCES IN OTHERS' BELIEF SYSTEMS

For example, we've had conversations about people who believe in God vs. people who don't. We try not to shy away from these conversations, even though they can be tough, at times. It's beautiful that our kids face diversity every day, and we want to make sure we arm them with the tools to stand firm in the belief system that they are developing while respecting the right of others to do so as well. It can be a tough balance, so we revisit this conversation often.

The preschool that David and Joshua attended was operated by owners who had a different cultural and religious beliefs than we did. This introduced many opportunities for discussion with our very young sons. One of the things that became obvious to us in that season is that young children have very open hearts and minds. Rather than try to avoid the many questions that they had about the differences, we chose to engage them with the goal of setting the foundation for them to interact with others and show love and respect. Don't run away from the touchy conversations. They're going to form their thoughts from somewhere. Let it be with your influence.

TEACH THEM ABOUT OUR FAITH FROM A PLACE OF LOVE FOR GOD, NOT HATE FOR OTHERS OR FROM A PLACE OF FEAR

We aim to teach our children that the foundation of our faith is God's love towards us. Hatred or judgment towards others does not make us righteous towards God. In teaching God-centered faith, we hope to instill in them the desire to live out God's plan for their lives and to avoid the trap of comparing themselves to others as a measure of how "good" they are.

Encourage Them to Study and Learn the Bible for Themselves

Strengthen their own faith vs. regurgitating what Mommy and Daddy tell them. As our children grow older, the ability to comprehend new information grows by leaps and bounds. As such, we arm them with the tools to move at their own pace. In our home, this includes many children's bibles; more than we can count, at every reading level, in English and Spanish. (Our children are learning Spanish, as well.)

It's not uncommon for the kids to take one of their Bible books to bed with them and read stories on their own before falling asleep at night. They're developing their own desire to learn and study God's Word.

Engage in Regular Discussions about Preferences and the Importance of Respecting Others' Rights to Make a Different Decision

Not everything is a matter of principle. Some things are a matter of preference. As an example, we made the decision early on that we would not celebrate the tradition of Santa Claus during Christmas. Not because we believe that others are wrong for doing so, but because we choose to celebrate differently. Our conversations about our Christmas celebration preferences often include discussion about not feeling like everyone else must share our preferences. We think this is an important lesson for them to understand. The world is filled with people with different belief systems, even within groups that share religious faiths.

Call to Action:
Purchase your child a bible with the appropriate reading level. Encourage him/her to read it for themselves.

Acceptance/Love
Chapter 2

Create an Environment of Love in the Home

We make it palpable. Love is felt in everything from meals to discipline. Peaceful. We feel so strongly that our immediate family should be a source of love and support for all members in it. Let's face it; the world can be harsh at times. We all need a place to retreat. An ear to bend. A shoulder to cry on. We intentionally provide that for our children. We want them to know that they can always be unfiltered, unguarded, 100% themselves here, and be loved and accepted.

HAVE GROUND RULES

No shouting (nice speech). No fighting, slamming doors, etc. Treat others with kindness. This is a non-negotiable in our home. And this didn't start as just rules for the children. This started as non-negotiables in our marriage; to treat one another with kindness and respect. Honor. Then it spilled over into our children.

We don't have a list of rules posted somewhere in our home. (But that's a great idea!) For us, it's more of a general tone that's known around our home. We began teaching this early in their lives. Some of the teaching includes verbal direction (and redirection), but most of the teaching has been through example. They've fallen in line with the tone of the home, and we have set the tone as their parents.

Meals Together – Discussion Around the Dinner Table

We wish we could do this for every meal. Unfortunately for us, and many other families, it simply isn't the case. However, as frequently as we can, we do. Additionally, when we can eat together, we do it without the distraction of devices, etc. Television off. Phones put away. No iPads at the table. Just family, food, and conversation. It's a great way to stay connected.

We've heard the former first family of the United States, President and Mrs. Obama describe their dinnertime ritual of "Roses and Thorns." During dinner, they along with their daughters, discuss the highs and lows of their day. This really resonated with us and we try to implement this practice with our children as well. Right now, because they're so young, the conversation often takes unexpected, and often comical turns. However, we believe we're setting the foundation and getting them used to engaging in rich discussion as a family.

Showing Genuine Interest in What's Important to Them

Being dismissed as unimportant feels terrible. As adults, we often see it as disrespectful. Our children can receive it as being shunned. And it can cause them to shut down. We try to keep in mind that while they're young, we're setting the tone for the engagement that we'll have with them moving forward. We want to make it easy for them to come to us with the "big stuff." So, we have to set the stage with the "little stuff."

Engage Them in Things That Are Important to Us

We try to be intentional about including the children when possible in things like exercising, or even family goal planning. It's important to us that they feel like important parts of our unit. This also helps them see themselves as a part of something bigger than themselves. For example, like most parents, we celebrate small milestones and accomplishments in the lives of our children. First day of swimming class! Giving a speech at school!

We recently realized that we weren't giving that same level of attention and celebration to our milestones and accomplishments. Or at least, not in a way that the children could recognize it and celebrate with us. So now we celebrate as a family when Daddy successfully completes a project at work, or when Mommy gets special recognition on her job. We're teaching them to give love and support, in addition to receiving it for themselves.

CALL TO ACTION:

Make a priority to eat together regularly. Start with one time per week. Increase over time.

Verbal Reassurance

FULLY ENGAGED GREETINGS EACH DAY

Mornings, reunion at the end of the day (us-them, them – each other). We remember hearing Gayle King and Oprah Winfrey once discussing how Gayle would stop whatever she was doing when her children entered the room and greeted them with excitement. We thought, "Wow! That must make them feel very valued." We want our children to feel like that, also. We want them to know that they are important and that we're genuinely happy to see them each day. We try to be intentional in not taking them for granted and giving a passive greeting on "autopilot." We greet them fully engaged… eye contact, genuine smile, warm hugs.

ONE ON ONE OPPORTUNITIES TO "POUR INTO THEM"

Tell them how thankful we are to have them. Let them hear us thank God for them. These moments happen spontaneously, and they love it. Whenever we have a moment alone with one of them, whether sitting on the sofa, helping prepare for the day or cuddling before sleep at night, we'll take a minute (most of the time, literally just one minute) and tell them how much we appreciate having them in our lives. There's always time to show gratitude. And it also serves as a reminder to us. We really are fortunate to have these wonderful children.

ALLOW THEM TO HEAR US TELL EACH OTHER HOW WONDERFUL WE THINK THEY ARE – NOT JUST FOR SOMETHING GOOD THAT THEY'VE DONE

Sometimes when we know they're within earshot, we'll say to one another something positive about the children. For example, "Terence, have you noticed how kind David is? I stopped and thought about it today. I'm so thankful for his kind spirit." Don't get us wrong; we have these conversations authentically anyway. But watched the boys walk into the building, Terence realized that he really hurt Joshua's feelings when he snapped at him. Before he went to work that morning, he called Joshua's classroom and asked him for forgiveness. When speaking to his teacher later, she informed us that that the conversation that morning had changed Joshua's entire demeanor and he went on to have a great day.

Apologizing to our children does not diminish our parental authority in any way. In fact, it's been our experience that it strengthens it. There's strength in humility. It doesn't take anything away from us to acknowledge to our children that we're human. And that we make mistakes, too. Additionally, it provides them with a model of how they should handle it when they've hurt or offended someone.

Teach Them about God's Grace Through the Grace that We Demonstrate to Others

We use those someone-needs-forgiveness moments as opportunities to talk about God's grace. Our goal with these conversations is to help them see the parallel of how God extends grace to us when we've messed up, just as we're often called upon to extend grace to others. This practice of helping them put themselves in the shoes of others plants the seeds of empathy and helps them see that they, too, are sometimes in need of forgiveness. Over time, we believe this practice will also help them see how loving and forgiving God is of them. Of course, this is a great lesson for us as well.

Teach Them to Ask for Forgiveness When They've Wronged Someone and Quickly Forgive When They've Been Wronged

The operative word here is quickly. We'll admit that throughout our lives, we've had many instances of letting offenses fester too long without asking for forgiveness. We've also been guilty of not forgiving others, holding grudges. In fact, we'll admit that we still struggle with this. We don't want our kids to have the same struggle. The irony of this is that as we've observed them over the years so far, forgiving others is something that they do naturally and very easily. In fact, it is we who are learning from them, how to forgive. We pray that they don't lose that as they get older.

Allow Them to See Us Apologize and Forgive Each Other When They Witness Us Disagree or "Bump Heads"

We often marvel at how intimate this "family life" is. Our kids see us at our best, our worst, and various points in between. As such, they have witnessed an occasional disagreement between the two of us. Fortunately, we resolved early in our marriage to fight fair, so our disagreements are generally long discussions laced with exasperated sighs. Nonetheless, our kids are aware that we have such disagreements, and we don't mind them seeing healthy conflict. For one, it helps them have a realistic perspective of what a healthy marriage is – not perfect. It also provides an opportunity to demonstrate how to resolve healthy conflict. We're very intentional about allowing them to see us apologize to each other. It's important to us that they witness the humility, love, and respect that we have for one another. Our prayer is that they model that in their future relationships, as well.

Call to Action:

Next time parents have a verbal disagreement in front of the kids, allow them to witness the apology and forgiveness.

Enforce the "Team Houston" Concept

Sometimes During Family Game Time, We're All on the Same Team – We All Win

We are a "game night" family. We think it's a great way to have a fun, inexpensive evening while strengthening our family bonds. However, our crew can be quite competitive, which isn't necessarily a bad thing. But sometimes, we find that the "I win, you lose" concept can be rubbed in a little too harshly. So occasionally, we'll play a game and choose to all be on the same team. An occasional reminder that ultimately, we share the same success.

Teach Them to Celebrate the Accomplishments of Each Other

We had an episode recently where David came home with a progress report that Joshua didn't have. Given that David's report was extremely positive, we heaped on the praise, which saddened Joshua to the point of tears. As we talked to him, he expressed that he was sad because David had a report and he didn't, and he wanted to receive the same celebration that David was receiving. We explained to our wonderful little Joshua that sometimes David would have successes that he won't have, and sometimes he would have successes that David won't have. We explained further that they both had to learn to celebrate the successes of each other; to be happy when someone we love is happy.

The next day when Joshua brought his progress report home, we all celebrated him for his great report, especially David. He learned the lesson from Joshua's experience the day before. Be happy for others, especially those that you love. Celebrate others
and give them the opportunity to celebrate with you.

Teach Them to Encourage Each Other and Cheer Each Other On

We often have times of forming a circle, placing someone in the middle of the circle while the rest of the family crowds around them and tells them all the wonderful things that we can think of about them while showering them with kisses. We do this once a week, sometimes more, specifically if one of the children requests it. We often go in reverse birth order, with everyone taking a turn in the middle, even Mommy and Daddy.

It's a wonderful experience to be showered with love and affirmation. We believe it's one of the things that really sets a tone of love and acceptance in our home. It's building the foundation of them knowing that no matter what harshness or rejection they receive from the outside world, there's love and acceptance within these four walls. Not only is it a blessing for the receiver of the affirmation but also for those that speak the words of love, as well. By speaking these words, we remind ourselves of what's good about one another. It strengthens our bond in indescribable ways.

Intentional Family Times that We All Participate In

No one is left out. If someone isn't there, it's not complete. We wait. This sends the message to them that we're all a part of this unit. Our family times are so very simple. Various kinds of games… Uno, matching games, various board games. A movie on Netflix. No need to spend tons of money or make a big spectacle of it as long as we're all together. We believe that in the end, it's the little consistent things that they'll remember most about their childhood.

Call to Action:

Intentionally devote a specific time for family time – weekly game night, movie night… Flexibility may be required to make sure everyone can participate.

Importance of Loving Others

TREAT OTHERS WITH KINDNESS AND RESPECT

This is a non-negotiable in our home. We model it with the way we treat each other and the children, and we expect them to follow suit. We encourage them to be the ones to set the example for their peers at school in the way they treat their teachers and fellow students. We also talk to them about people with different physical and mental abilities. We encourage them to ask us questions to help them process their understanding of these differences and how they can empathize and treat everyone with kindness and sensitivity.

NO BULLYING

Ever. Completely unacceptable. This is another non-negotiable in our home. We talk about it in terms they understand. Recently, we were discussing how people joke with one another. And we told them, "If you're joking around with someone, but they're not welcoming the jokes or having fun with the situation, that's not funny, that's just mean." This opened up an entire discussion about various instances they've experienced at school that fit that scenario. They were surprised when we told them that teasing and making fun of people is a form of bullying. They seemed to have thought that only physical assaults constitute bullying. We teach them what bullying is and set very clear boundaries for them. We are teaching them that they are also not to tolerate anyone bullying them. They're still rather young, so we know that we'll continue to be on this journey for quite some time, but we feel it's important to lay the foundation now regarding what is acceptable behavior for them, and for those they allow in their lives.

CONSIDER THE FEELINGS OF OTHERS

Encourage them to think about how their words/behaviors affect others. We don't know if it's possible to teach empathy or emotional intelligence. However, we do believe there's something powerful about awareness. And it's been our experience, unfortunately, that so many of us go through life without the awareness of how our words and behaviors affect other people. We know we've been guilty of this! We cringe even now when we consider some of the insensitive comments we've made or the oblivious nature by which we've gone on about life while not realizing the impact we were having on others. Of course, we've been on the receiving end of hurt, as well, and often find ourselves thinking, "Wow! Why would (s)he do that to me?" Well, we recognize that the truth is, they weren't thinking of us at all.

We don't have the expectation that our children will be perfect in the way they interact with others. That's not even the goal. We simply understand the value of a kind word instead of a harsh one, a genuine smile vs. a haughty look. We just want them to know that they can be a light in the world, and we hope that they learn to use their words and energy intentionally instead of being reckless and hurtful without even realizing the hurtful impact they could be having on others.

Create Opportunities for Them to Serve Others – Raising Unselfish Children in a Selfish World

During our pregnancy with the boys, our women's ministry leader gifted us with a book called "Raising Unselfish Children in a Selfish World." We devoured that book like a meal! We couldn't put it down. The theme of the book resonated with us. Not from a place of wanting to raise some perfect beings that would someday be candidates to be canonized as saints, but truly from a place of wanting all of us as a family to really live out the values that we say we believe… loving our neighbor as ourselves.

The best advice we can give about teaching your children to serve is to lead by example. Sure, we teach them things that we think are important for them to incorporate into how they think about serving people, but as the old saying goes, "More is caught than taught." Honestly, the most impactful lessons they get from us about serving others is the way they witness us serving others. Whether it's our aging parents, strangers, friends/other family members, or each other, they see service as just a way of life. Our commitment to service, whether domestic or abroad, has impacted them so strongly, that they now develop their own ideas about how they would like to help people. We truly pray that this is one of the attributes they carry with them throughout their lives.

Call to Action:

Allow them to participate in the next charitable donation (i.e., Goodwill drop off)

Prioritizing the Marriage
Chapter 3

Model Healthy Affections between Mom & Dad

ALLOW THEM TO SEE MOMMY AND DADDY HUG

Just as we hug and dote on them, we hug and dote on each other. We want them to know that we hold each other as a priority. In no way does that minimize the prioritization we place on them.

ALLOW THEM TO SEE GENUINE AFFECTION BETWEEN MOM AND DAD

Don't shy away from showing them the teenage-ish giggles and playfulness, etc. In other words, they see us for who we are, and not some image of what "mature marriage" is supposed to be. It's fine and even desirable for them to witness the "realness" of our marriage. The joy and laughter that we experience with each other. Our marriage is not merely some partnership for parenting them. We really enjoy each other. And we allow our children to see us in the context of Terence & Eardie, the couple, not just Daddy & Mommy, the parents.

TEACH BOUNDARIES LIKE KNOCKING ON THE BEDROOM DOOR TO ASK FOR ENTRY VS. BARGING IN

For obvious reasons, we lock our door at night to prevent unexpected visitors from entering. Although they don't yet know why, they do know that it is expected that they knock, identify themselves, and ask for permission to come in. This sends the message to them that our bedroom is "Mommy & Daddy" space.

Teach Them the Sanctity of Our Bed

No sleeping in our bed... well, most of the time! We confess that we don't always get this one right, especially with our baby girl. But for the most part, we do try to keep our kids out of our bed. Of course, there are exceptions for a sick child or the occasional bad dream, but generally speaking, they know that Mommy and Daddy's bed is for Mommy and Daddy.

Call to Action:

While watching TV or a movie as a family, mom and dad practice sitting in a cuddle. Allow the children to become used to seeing you embrace if they haven't already.

Make Date Night a Priority

We must confess, this is an area that we fall short in, repeatedly. Between work, parenting, passion projects, ministry, etc., we find it extremely difficult to make date night a priority. A very real barrier for us is child care. Not having family living in-state, we rely on paid childcare services. After paying for childcare for both of us to work outside of the home, we sometimes don't budget enough to pay for childcare for regular date nights. We've found that the cost of childcare can exceed the cost of the date itself! Nonetheless, we do recognize the importance of carving out time for just the two of us. We're constantly looking for ways to do this creatively, to overcome the barriers that would otherwise prevent us from having this precious alone time.

Find a Trusted Friend, Family Member or Babysitter to Ensure Opportunities to have One-on-One Time Without the Children

If having a friend or family member babysit occasionally is an option, don't be shy about asking for and receiving help. In the past, we've even swapped childcare with another couple with small children. We would take turns babysitting for each other so that we could each have date nights while knowing that our children are safe and having fun.

Adhere to/Enforce Firm Bedtime Schedule to Ensure Quiet One-on-One Time in the Evenings

In the absence of true "date nights," this tends to be our default. Oftentimes, our date nights consist of getting the children down early and watching a movie on television while munching on some snacks that we've managed to get into the house without our children noticing. Quiet, alone time is what matters most. If date night is a night in, it's better than nothing.

Consider Lunch Dates as an Alternative If Childcare is an Issue

Lunchtime is a great time to connect, particularly for couples that may not have childcare options available for evenings out. Remember, the important thing here is to connect. Try not to get caught up in what a date should look like. Just make the best of the opportunities that you have.

Ensure that You Have – or are Working Towards Having – a Schedule that Allows for Adequate Rest, Not Just for Kids but also for Parents

With so many things competing for time and energy, families are often overscheduled, overworked, and stressed. Make it a priority to assess what activities could be minimized to make time for adequate rest, and time together. It's likely that you respond better to each other when you're not tired. This may help with your day-to-day interactions with each other and increase your ability to seek out moments of connectivity.

Call to Action:

Plan a date night for the upcoming week. If childcare is an issue, prepare the children for an early bedtime and plan a quiet evening in. No heavy conversations, just connect. Watch a movie or your favorite show.
Just the two of you.

Establish Healthy Communication with Your Spouse

∞

The cornerstone to modeling a healthy relationship is actually having a healthy relationship. Communication is said to be one of the leading challenges for many couples. Once children are in the picture, it becomes increasingly important to communicate well and work together as partners.

DEAL WITH CONFLICT IN A HEALTHY WAY

Practice discussion and negotiation instead of arguing. Not only is this important for your children, but it's important as a foundation for any married couple, or any relationship in general. Many of us were not taught how to handle conflict in a healthy way. It is possible to address problems within the marriage in a healthy, loving way, with both parties feeling heard, loved, and respected, even while we encourage each other to grow and improve. A good practice is to mutually establish a non-negotiable rule of no disrespect when communicating with one another. No shouting, cursing, belittling, or any other toxic behavior. Instead, practice healthy communication behaviors like empathetic listening, compromise, and respect.

SET ASIDE TIME FOR REGULAR CHECK-IN MEETINGS

One of the strategies that we've implemented in our marriage has been intentionally spending at least 100 minutes of uninterrupted time together per week. We challenge ourselves to carve out this time with no distractions to just talk and connect with each other. No talking about bills or kids, just focusing on how we're doing individually and as a couple. At first thought, 100 minutes per week didn't sound like a lot to us, but we were surprised to realize that we don't naturally spend this amount of quality time together consistently. Being purposeful has changed that tremendously. Also, have expanded family meetings so the children can participate.

DEVELOP A REGULAR PRAYER ROUTINE WHERE YOU TWO PRAY TOGETHER AS A COUPLE

This is such an intimacy-building act, particularly when done consistently. We were introduced to a model format by a more seasoned couple that we respect. The husband begins the prayer with thanksgiving and covering his wife and family in prayer. Then presents his personal concerns to the Lord. The wife then covers her husband's prayer concerns with a prayer of her own and then presents her concerns to the Lord. The husband then wraps up the prayer by covering his wife's concerns that she has just expressed.

Praying together allows couples to share their concerns and hear each other's heart. There's something special and intimate about going to God together to petition Him together. Also, hearing your spouse's prayer requests now arms you with what you need to continue praying for your spouse long after you leave that prayer closet.

Make Major Decisions Together

Consider one another. As we encourage other couples, it's pretty common to hear someone share frustrations regarding their spouse making a major purchase without considering them. Or agreeing to lend money or provide long-term housing for a loved one. In order to go deeper in your attempt to strengthen your marriage, it's important that you consider your spouse when making decisions that affect the household. Making major decisions together really helps to build trust within the relationship as you each get more and more information about how your spouse processes information and make decisions.

Call to Action:
Pray together tonight while embracing, using the format described earlier in this chapter. Husband begins. Wife follows. Husband closes.

Maintain a Balanced Schedule – Don't Overschedule

It is extremely difficult to maintain a prioritized marriage when both husband and wife are running all over town like crazy people. Work, extra work activities/projects, homework, after-school activities, class parties, playdates... We could go on, but we think you get the point. We're doing too much. And then whenever we return home, we're exhausted and depleted, oftentimes, without feeling like we have anything to give to anyone. Understandably, there may be certain seasons that require such intense activity, but intentional effort should be made to not make this the norm.

Keep a Family Calendar to Ensure Both Parents are Aware of Schedule to Avoid Scheduling Conflicts

Imagine how many missed appointments, disappointments or arguments would be avoided with having a centralized calendar that each family member can access. Using this tool to schedule doctor's appointments, work travel and important events/meetings not only provides clear direction for what is to be expected but it also gives transparency and accountability to whether you are making your spouse a priority.

Too Many Activities Tire Out the Children and the Parents

Limit activities to what is reasonable for your family. As parents, we need to learn how to say no when it comes to guarding our time. Whether it's an abundance of social activities, or even service commitments, some weeks, we tire ourselves out and leave no room for rest. Inadvertently, we teach our children to do the same. Parents commonly fill up children's calendars with sports, lessons, and playdates. If we're not intentional, we may find that we're constantly on the go. Instead, consider setting limits on the number of activities engaged in on a weekly basis. Busyness can cause us to miss opportunities to connect as a family and also to teach children the power of rest, reflection, and rejuvenation.

Schedule a Season of Stillness

We are intentional about identifying a few weeks each year when all (or most) extra-curricular activities cease and the family can refocus and reconnect. We find that for our family, the best time to have these periods of stillness is during the summer and/or over the Christmas holiday season. Taking a family vacation is a great way to have intentional stillness, by stepping away from the daily grind of life and creating moments where you are able to assess whether current activities should be continued or discontinued. Even if a vacation is not in the budget, taking an intentional pause can allow you to assess what's working for the family and whether the time spent participating in a particular activity is consuming valuable moments that could otherwise be beneficial for the overall health of the family.

Set Reasonable Goals for Mom and Dad, Professionally and Financially

Over-working is not healthy. In many families, both parents have careers outside of the home. For many, balancing work life and home life presents challenges, and isn't always easy. At times, one of the roles (either work life or home life) may suffer. In some instances, it may be necessary to revisit career goals and see how they may be adapted to balance better the many roles we tend to have in life. Is it possible to work a few days a week remotely? Or even job share? During times when an important project is demanding more time, is it possible to get additional support from family or a nanny to make sure that the children continue to have the consistency that they need? What adjustments can be made either at work or at home to ensure that the most important priorities remain just that? Be realistic and flexible.

Call to Action:

Review schedule this month and see what activities can be removed from the schedule to free up some time that can be re-allocated as couple time.

Maintain Healthy Engagement of Adult-Centered Activities

◇◇◇

Choose Some Vacations that are Family-Friendly, but not Fully Child-Focused

Yes, we've made a few visits to see the big mouse and his friends at his magic kingdom. However, we've also been very intentional about creating other experiences for our children that aren't centered around them. We find that they find fun wherever they are, so there's nothing wrong with choosing a vacation that we will enjoy just as much as they will.

Find Ways to Serve Together to Aid in Staying Connected

Whether serving our family (chores, routine home duties) or serving outside of the home (volunteer efforts, mission work, etc.), serving together helps us stay connected and remain centered as we focus on things outside of ourselves. As a bonus, we're also modeling behavior for our children that we hope they will emulate as they get older.

Come Together with Other Couples at a Similar Stage For Regular Fellowship

During various seasons of our marriage, we've found it quite helpful to enjoy regular fellowship with other couples that are in a similar stage of life as we are. These connections help to encourage our marriage and learn from other couples while providing a healthy social balance. Oftentimes, since the other couples are at a similar stage, bringing the children along is encouraged, to minimize the childcare barrier.

Expose Kids to/Teach Them to Enjoy Some Activities that You Enjoy

In addition to playing games and enjoying activities that the children enjoy, we also encourage them to engage in activities that we enjoy. One example in our home is jigsaw puzzles. Although one child has shown a very small interest in jigsaw puzzles, the other two have neither patience nor interest in puzzles. However, it is one of Mommy's favorite activities. Therefore, when choosing fun-night activities, puzzles are a part of the rotation. No, the children don't love it, but they've learned that it's a part of the rotation. Just as each of them gets to choose a fun activity that they enjoy, Mommy and Daddy get to choose an activity too. And we all participate. It teaches them that Mommy and Daddy have interests outside of the things that they want to do.

Call to Action:

Before planning your next trip to a theme park, consider choosing a vacation that the adults would enjoy as much as the children.

Protection/Boundaries/Safety
Chapter 4

With so many forces within our culture threatening harm to our children, it's important to be intentional about protecting them.

Teaching Them to Honor Their Personal Boundaries

∞

We believe that even small children should have personal boundaries that are honored and respected. We believe that even now we are setting standards in their lives for using their voices and expressing their limitations. We want them to feel confident enough to both establish their boundaries and to speak up when they feel their boundaries are threatened.

Don't Ever Force Them to Hug/Embrace Anyone They Don't Want To

This sometimes causes us to face some very raised eyebrows. Whether it's aunts, uncles, grandparents, or whomever, if they are reluctant to hug or show affection to someone, we don't force, or even encourage them to. We teach them to not ignore the things that make them feel uncomfortable to please others. And we also demonstrate to them that we support them over anyone else, always. We believe that it's important to sow these seeds early in their life, in hopes that it will become their normal to use their voices and enforce their boundaries at all times.

Have Age-Appropriate Conversations about Private Areas and Appropriate/Inappropriate Touching

We began these conversations when our children were as young as age two. Like many parents, those earliest lessons centered around "good touch / bad touch." As the children get older, the conversations grow with them and develop into teaching them how to set boundaries for themselves regarding other people touching them. Like other parents, we have found that bath time is an ideal time for those conversations. Additionally, we look for other opportunities to pepper them with this information, as well.

We try to avoid lecturing them regarding this or anything else, but rather give them information in small doses. In order to do this effectively, we recognize that we must try our best to be prepared to answer any awkward questions they may have with honesty and in a matter-of-fact way that they can understand. This helps establish a foundation of communication within the family that we pray will strengthen as the children grow older.

Have Real Conversations about Them Speaking Up for Their Preferences

Don't just "go along to get along." We teach the kids that their opinions matter. When interacting with their peers or others, they should make up their minds about things rather than just going along with the crowd. Within our home, they are encouraged to ask questions for understanding and to think about how they feel about requests being made of them. Obviously, this doesn't give them a license to defy requests that we make of them as parents, but we are seeking to teach them to speak up when something doesn't feel right to them internally.

Have Real Conversations about How Valuable They Are to God and Their Parents

Teach them the importance of valuing themselves. We tell our children repeatedly how much we love them and how much God loves them. We teach them that they are valuable to God, to us, and that they should value themselves as well. We hope that this contributes to developing a strong, positive self-esteem and that they will not believe outside narratives that seek to convince them otherwise.

Call to Action:

Make sure you're establishing real boundaries and enforcing them. It is important that this behavior is modeled.

No Secrets

Consistently Teach Them that If Someone Asks Them to Keep a Secret, Say No!

This has been a non-negotiable rule within our home with all caregivers, extended family members, etc. We teach them not to keep secrets. We felt it was important to set this foundation because "keeping a secret" can be one of the tools that violators tend to use with little children. We thought it was important to develop a habit of them sharing information with us, particularly while they're young and lack the judgment to determine what they should or should not hold as secret. Just tell everything!

When They Go Through the Phase of Telling On Each Other, Resist the Urge to Scold Them for Telling or to Tell Them to "Stop Snitching"

Once they start holding back information, you can't expect them at a young age to always have the judgment to know what to share, and what not to. Encourage them to talk as much as they want and you, the adult, sort it out.

Teach Them the Proper Name for Body Parts and Talk Plainly and Openly

Don't allow a culture of shame to develop regarding their body. This did produce a lot of laughter amongst our extended family earlier on as they heard very small people speak of "penis" and "vagina." Our rationale for that was that we wanted them to feel comfortable talking about things plainly and not having shame associated with them. This makes it easier for them to tell us when something hurts, or something feels uncomfortable.

SHARE THIS WITH OTHER FAMILY/CAREGIVERS SO THAT THEY DON'T SEND A MIXED MESSAGE

We have been very intentional about sharing these practices with caregivers and family members that interact with the children regularly. We've done this in an effort to increase consistency in the messaging that the children receive. We've found that our village mostly came alongside us in our efforts to set this foundation once we actively communicated with them. But we had to be willing to have those conversations.

CALL TO ACTION:

Look for opportunities to have a brief "teaching moment" to remind them not to keep secrets. Not a lecture. "Pepper them with the information."

Careful Entrusting Them to Others

Screen Caregivers Carefully

Obviously, parents can't control every circumstance; it is often necessary to leave our children in the care of others. Take as much precaution as possible in choosing caregivers, whatever that looks like for the individual situation – background checks, recommendations/ referrals, observation tools, etc.

Must be Driven Around in Our Vehicle

Up to date maintenance, car seats properly installed, etc. It's common practice for our family that whoever has our children, has access to our family vehicle. Practically speaking, only certain vehicles can accommodate three small children, with car seats and all of their other gear. We've been asked, "Aren't you concerned about someone else driving your vehicle? What if they get into an accident?" Well, our answer to that is, if we trust someone enough to care for our most prized "possessions," our children, they generally have access to other things that are less important. And secondly, we understand the risk of accident, etc. Yes, things happen. But we feel better knowing that if something unfortunate like that does happen, there's a better chance to minimize risk with a properly maintained vehicle, properly installed car seats, etc.

Be Explicit Regarding Expectations While in Care of Others

Don't assume everyone knows. Communication is very important. Keep in mind that everyone does things differently with their children. That's not to say their way is "wrong," but we continue to make it clear that we have specific expectations of anyone that spends significant time with our children. Again, as parents, we can't be afraid to have difficult or awkward conversations regarding our children.

Ask Children for Feedback and LISTEN

Trust your instinct if something seems off. We ask our children questions about even the smallest details of their lives and then practice listening to them. This is helpful to get us used to listening to them, and it also helps them see that we are very interested in what is happening with them. By staying connected, we're able to notice when their moods shift or if anything seems "off" with them. We're only able to do this by being engaged and really listening and paying attention to them.

Call to Action:

Have regular check-ins with your child's regular caregivers. Share reminders of expectations and invite feedback.

Have Technology Safeguards

USE CHILD PROTECTION MEASURES ON ALL DEVICES, TV SYSTEMS, ETC.

Make use of the password-required features on devices and programs that your children use (Netflix, etc.). There is a wide variety of software available that allows parents to monitor the internet/app usage of older children/teens that have their own devices. For smaller children, immediate supervision is a really good idea, when your child is using devices. As I've heard one educator say, "At any given time, there are several billion people on the internet. Would you allow your child to wander around real-time amongst several billion people unattended?" Be careful and don't take for granted that your child will always make the right decisions about what they view and who they interact with online. Exercise caution.

HAVE BLACKOUT TIMES FOR DEVICES

Have a crate/bowl/container in your bedroom that all devices must be placed in at a certain time. It's a good idea to monitor your child's use of technology, both for internet safety, and also to ensure that the children don't use devices excessively.

BE INTENTIONAL ABOUT TEACHING THEM THE PROPER USE OF TECHNOLOGY

Being "Good cybercitizens." Technology has changed the way we do things in the world. At this point, it's a mainstay in our world, and that's probably not going to change. With that in mind, it's important to teach them how to use computers, smartphones, tablets, etc. However, we must teach them to use the devices properly. Teach them not to be bullies and teach them about the negative side of "cyber footprints." Although there are many positives regarding the way technology enhances our lives, when used irresponsibly, the results can be very harmful.

Be Intentional about Maintaining Awareness of Latest Apps, etc.

Make every effort to know what your kids could be getting into. We won't pretend to be experts in that but know that there are parent information resources all over the internet to support parents in their attempts to implement internet safety practices with their children. Seek them out.

Call to Action:

Begin implementing a blackout time for devices. If they've grown accustomed to not having such boundaries, have a real conversation about doing something different that will be healthy and helpful to everyone. Be patient if there's resistance to the change. With time and consistency, they'll adapt.

Expect Good and Prepare for Bad

MAKE SURE THEY KNOW PROPER NAMES OF FAMILY MEMBERS AND IMPORTANT PHONE NUMBERS

Some of our earliest memories as children include learning important family information, such as our address and phone number. We would recite them over and over. We've passed this on to my children as well. As soon as they began talking, we began teaching them things like all of our names, our phone numbers, etc. It's important for them to know how to instruct someone to contact us, if necessary.

HAVE UNPLANNED DRILLS OF WHAT THEY SHOULD DO IN CASE OF AN EMERGENCY

We have lots of unplanned drills in our home. After we teach them things, like calling for help and hiding from intruders, we create opportunities for them to practice the things they've learned. Whether it's how to get out of a car seat and out of the car to yell for help or what to do if they can't wake up Mommy, we practice what they should do in case of emergencies.

HELP THEM UNDERSTAND THE IMPORTANCE OF FOLLOWING SAFETY RULES WITH FRANK AND HONEST, AGE-APPROPRIATE CONVERSATIONS ABOUT POTENTIAL CONSEQUENCES OF NOT FOLLOWING THE RULES

One evening during game night, both of our phones alarmed with an "Amber Alert." The kids were curious, so we frankly explained to them what the alarm represented, which launched into a conversation about kidnapping. What we learned from that discussion was how naïve children naturally are, and that they really do have to be taught safety measures. With the bubble that we've created for them, they just couldn't conceive the idea of harm coming their way. It made us wonder if we may be shielding them too much. At minimum, we must talk to them, in a way that they will understand, and teach them about dangers that we must guard against.

CALL TO ACTION:

Adopt short, simple, easy-to-remember phrases that they can hold onto and embrace. Example: our number one family vacation rule – STAY TOGETHER!

Structure/Discipline

Chapter 5

Our overall approach to discipline and creating structure for our children is centered around safety and teaching.

Discipline from a Place of Love, Not Anger

We provide structure for our children and discipline them because we love them. We recognize the importance of creating healthy barriers to protect them from danger. Likewise, we also know that it is important to correct behavior that can prove harmful to them long-term. We must teach them to make good decisions. Until they learn to make good decisions for themselves, it is important for them to obey our instruction, as we exercise good stewardship over them.

Do Not Discipline Them While We're Angry

This goes without saying. Giving children discipline while angry can lead to harsh voices, poor word choice, or worse. A best practice is that when you find yourself angry, retreat for a while until you're able to view the situation with a level head. When we're overcome with anger, it's easy to lose sight of the purpose of the overall discipline, which is to protect and teach them.

Focus on the Lesson

A good strategy of providing discipline with love is to focus on the lesson that the child should learn. Ask yourself if you're trying to punish them or trying to teach them. A punishment puts a heavier emphasis on consequences of the action, whereas a lesson places emphasis on teaching them an enduring message that will help them make better decisions next time.

Remind Them of Unconditional Love and Acceptance

Whenever we're correcting our children, we seek to be intentional about reminding them of our love for them. We let them know that while there are consequences for their unseemly behavior, it does not in any way diminish the love that we have for them. Also, be mindful to not (intentionally or unintentionally) withhold affection from children. Be careful not to send the message that love for them is tied to their behavior. We tell our children over and over again that we love them, regardless of what they do.

Remember the "Why"

When we create structure for our children, it isn't to "show them who's boss" or to exert power over them. The structure we create for them is for their safety while they're learning how to make sound decisions for themselves. Likewise, discipline is about correction and redirection, not about breaking their will. In our home, we try to bear in mind that the ultimate goal is to teach them the ways of the Lord in the hopes that when they are older, they will not depart from it.

Call to Action:

Make a commitment not to discipline your children while you're angry. Step away for a few minutes, or as long as it takes to deal with the issue with a spirit of love.

Be Consistent

SET EXPECTATIONS

One of the most important things parents can do to in the realm of correction and discipline is to set clear expectations for them. After all, how can they be held responsible for obeying rules that they're unaware of? The teaching should come before the discipline. Otherwise, the correction is sporadic and inconsistent. Help your child(ren) know what you expect of them, and what they can expect from you if those expectations are not fulfilled.

FOLLOW THROUGH

To be consistent is to follow through on what you say you're going to do. If you say they have to eat all of their food at dinner or they won't get a treat, stick with it. If not, it sends them the message that you don't mean what you say and that they don't have to take you seriously. Say what you mean and mean what you say.

FAIRNESS BETWEEN CHILDREN

If you have more than one child, it's important to display fairness between the children. This doesn't mean that the discipline for each child will be exactly the same, but there shouldn't be any glaring differences between the standards of behavior for one child versus another.

COMMUNICATE CHANGES

Maya Angelou once said, "When you know better, you do better." Sometimes as parents, we realize that perhaps there is a better way of doing something or maybe a certain rule that was in place no longer holds value. Have conversations with your children about it.

Not only does it send the message that Mommy & Daddy acknowledge that they're learning as they go, but it also alleviates any confusion in the child's mind regarding changes that are occurring in the rules.

Call to Action:

Establish specific ground rules regarding chores, behavior expectations, etc. Then have an age-appropriate conversation with your children about the rules to help them understand the expectations.

Give Grace

Make Room for Growth

Keep in mind that the overall purpose of structure and discipline is to teach them. As such, we should also bear in mind that they will make mistakes along the way. They must grow into individuals that make Godly decisions. It's not going to happen with the first teaching or maybe not even the 10th. But over time, with consistency, they will get there. Try to exercise patience and a lot of grace.

Acknowledge Efforts to Improve

Try to "catch them trying," and celebrate them for it. Baby steps towards progress still count as progress. Point it out to them when you see them making efforts to grow in an area that they have not yet mastered. Not only will this go a long way for their confidence, but it will also serve as a reminder to you of why you're doing this in the first place. To see your little one grow into a man/woman with sound judgment that honors God.

Use the Opportunity to Teach about God's Grace

There is an amazing parallel between the way we discipline our children and the way God disciplines us. Try having intentional conversations with your children about how God loves us so much that he directs and redirects us, just as parents do the same for their children. Teach them also how God shows us grace when we mess up, just as parents do for their children.

This is an excellent opportunity to remind them, and ourselves, about God's love for us and how He loves us in spite of our flaws and failures. This is an important lesson to teach them because eventually, they will no longer be under our care. We want them to make good decisions, not to please us, but to please God. The earlier we can point them towards obedience to Him, the better.

CALL TO ACTION:

Have an intentional conversation with your child about God's grace and how it applies to all of our lives when we make mistakes or bad choices.

Practice Self Awareness

RECOGNIZE THE PARALLEL BETWEEN THEM AND US – WITH GOD

We are believers that parenting, along with most other things in life, have a higher purpose than just the day to day responsibilities. We believe that one of these purposes is to help us see ourselves more clearly. Do you see yourself in your kids? It's funny how that works. We can't even retell all of the times one of our children has done something and reminded us so much of one of us. At times, it's hilarious, but sometimes, we must admit, it's humbling. In our children, we often see the parallel between their relationship with us (as their parents) and our relationship with God as our father… the way we sulk when things don't go our way. Our stubborn persistence. Our unnecessary fear of some adventures. This is what we find humbling. Many of the things we find ourselves correcting them for are things that we actually struggle with ourselves, albeit in a different form. But we see the parallel. It helps us empathize with them and have patience with them. Also, it helps us see ourselves more clearly and want to grow in those areas, as well.

PRACTICE HUMILITY

No longer are we in the era of "Do as I say, not as I do," which is something we often heard as a child when we were instructed to do things that seemed contradictory to what our guardians were living out. We recognize that it takes a great deal of humility to acknowledge to your child "I made a mistake, and I ask you to forgive me" or "I was wrong to do things that way." Although that's not always the example we saw in our families of origin, we now see the culture of grace and humility that the practice has created in our home. Our children are learning from us how to acknowledge and recover from mistakes.

Identify How We are Modeling Improper Behavior

One evening our twin sons, who were maybe aged three at the time, would not eat their dinner. After an extended evening of us unsuccessfully trying to convince them to eat their food, we finally wrapped up for the night. Daddy, however, decided with firmness that he was going to teach them a lesson and that they were going to eat the food, BECAUSE DADDY SAID SO. So, he wrapped up and refrigerated the meal, only to warm it and place it on the table the next morning for breakfast.

By this point, the situation had become a battle of wills. The boys were defiant, and Daddy was determined. At that moment, Mommy asked Daddy if we could immediately stop and pray. As we prayed, we were reminded that we hadn't eaten the healthy meal that we had unsuccessfully tried to feed the kids the night before. We had eaten something different.

Conviction. While we wanted them to eat this nutritious meal, we realize now that the best way to steer them in that direction isn't by dominance, but rather by example. Be careful of what we're modeling to our children. Keep in mind that we're always teaching them something, whether we intend to or not. If they're watching us provide improper models of behavior, we can't be surprised when they began to exhibit that behavior, as well.

Call to Action:

Ask God to reveal to you how you might be the source of exposure to inappropriate behaviors and/or attitudes for your child. Commit to turn from those ways and give your child a new example.

Individualized Approach for Each Child

Reject "Lazy Parenting"

Growing up, Mommy had a friend who was one of several children. It was always amazing to see how their mother customized correction for each of her children. She once said it was important not to be a "lazy parent," meaning that she and her husband put a lot of thought and energy into parenting each child the way that he/she requires. They paid very close attention to their children and knew how to reward them best and how to redirect them best. We've tried to learn from that example and practice that since becoming parents.

Fair but Not Necessarily Equal

While the rules are consistent for all of our children, the reward/correction system is not identical for all of the children. It's important to study your children and know the things that they value and enjoy. Then you can tailor the structure and/or correction to what would be most impactful for them. As individuals, we're motivated by different things. That includes children. With that in mind, we try not to take a "one size fits all" approach to parenting them.

When They Get in Trouble Together, We Try to Find an Opportunity To Still Connect with Them One-on-One

In a home with three children, it's very common that finding trouble is a group endeavor. And while they may all get reprimanded together, we do commonly seek opportunities to connect with them individually, as well. One reason is to seek to steer them away from "group-think" where they develop the behavior of going along with the crowd. We want to avoid that. Also, we connect with them individually because we want to make sure we get just a few moments in for some individual teaching, specifically tailored to how we know they best receive information.

CALL TO ACTION:

In your (prayer) journal, write down your prayer requests for each child individually, by name. Identify areas that they need to improve upon and ask God for wisdom concerning how you may help them in their growth.

Chapter 6

Fun

Intentional Family Time

◇◇◇

With so many things competing for our attention, we have to be very intentional about carving out time for our family to have bonding time. That means making every effort to be efficient at work so that we can pull away and be fully present for quality family time.

GAME NIGHT

Our kids absolutely love game night, and we do, too. We play the traditional favorites (Monopoly, Uno, Scrabble, etc.) and we sometimes make up games, too. It's a great way to engage with them, talk to them about random stuff in their world, and they learn things without realizing it, too!

MAXIMIZE THE ROUTINES

Sometimes, we find time for silliness on the commute to school with silly songs and jokes. Bedtime stories are sometimes read dramatically, with disguised voices and animated facial expressions. Bath time is full of bubbles and giggles. In short, there's always time for fun.

OCCASIONAL FUN OUTINGS

This is one area that we recognize room for growth in our family.

After the craziness of work, school, extra-curricular activities, Mommy and Daddy are exhausted. However, we realize that the kids very much appreciate the occasional night out at the movies or a visit to the nearby indoor funhouse. In other words, kid-centric activities. Seeing how much they enjoy it makes us drag ourselves out to Chuck E. Cheese occasionally. Very small doses.

Relax the Rules Sometimes

Over time, we've created quite a bit of structure for our children. Limited television time during the week. Strict bedtime. Restricted unhealthy snacks. But sometimes, we do toss caution to the wind and let them watch television while eating snacks after bedtime. It's not frequent, but it does happen occasionally. Sometimes we all just need to unwind.

Call to Action:

Plan a game night with your family. Just a fun evening in on the living room floor with some age-appropriate favorites like Memory Game, Uno, Scrabble, etc.

Having Times with No Agenda

Like many families, we often find ourselves overscheduled, overspent, and overwhelmed. Too many activities and not enough time. Sometimes, we just need a period of time with nothing to do.

We Try as Much as We Can to Not Overschedule Our Weekends

We like to have at least one day over the weekend that we don't have anything planned. This means saying no to birthday parties and other social gatherings so that we can be intentional about having downtime to spend time together as a family and do absolutely nothing.

Summer Break

Over the summer, we plan a month in the summer when the children are removed from all of the extra activities (sports, Kumon, etc.) and have nothing to do but play outside, play games, watch movies, and just be kids. It's a break for them, and a break for us, as well. Nothing to practice. Nothing to be late for. It's quite liberating.

Work Hard, Play Hard

During the school year, our children's school gives a "homework packet" with the assignments for the week all at once. The packet comes home on Monday and is due back on Friday. It didn't take the children long to realize that if they did their homework early in the week, it would free up their evenings later in the week. Win, win for all of us. They're motivated to work hard when they get their homework, and we all get to catch our breaths a little as the week progresses.

Call to Action:

Take a look at your schedule and see what day you can find in the next month to do absolutely nothing. Block it off and protect it by not accepting any invitations. Just spend time together as a family doing nothing.

Family Vacations

AS FREQUENTLY AS POSSIBLE

We try to get away as a family a couple of times a year. For us, we value this time as a time to connect without so many of the distractions that we have to balance at home. Sometimes the trips are a couple hours' drive away; sometimes they're more elaborate, but what's most important is that we make time for them and protect that time as just family time. For us, that means we don't invite friends and other families along. It's a time of bonding just for us.

BALANCE OF CHILD-CENTRIC VS. NON-CHILD-CENTRIC

Over the years, we've been intentional about balancing our vacation experiences between trips that are child-focused (i.e., Disney, etc.) and fun, and cultural vacations into which we can incorporate some kid experiences. Every family is different, but for us, the preference is to expose them to diverse experiences to show them fun outside of typical child-focused activities. It's fun for the entire family, and they get to learn and stretch themselves in the process!

REVISIT THE VACATION AFTER THE VACATION

We often have so much fun reliving previous vacations through pictures or funny memories. Sometimes talking about our experiences creates an entirely new experience by itself and allows us to share even more joy.

CALL TO ACTION:

Plan your next family vacation. Get the kids involved. Keep in mind it doesn't have to be grand to be fun. What matters is that it allows for family bonding and fun!

Intentionally Choose Joy

WE LAUGH TOGETHER A LOT

As we complete this book project, our sons are now at the age where they're repeatedly trying to tell us knock-knock jokes. Their silliness is contagious. And we welcome all of it. Their giggles remind us of what is really important.

MAKE THE MUNDANE, MAGNIFICENT

During a recent visit to Orlando to see "The Big Mouse," we were greeted by an exceptionally long line for one of the rides that the kids definitely wanted to experience. We cautioned them, "Ok, but we're going to have to wait for a while before we get to the front of the line. We don't want to hear any complaining. We have to keep having fun even while we wait." And then we proceeded to play a series of games that kept us giggling and laughing, to the bemusement of our fellow park-goers. They couldn't believe that our children were having so much fun, even while waiting in line. It's really about choosing joy, even when complaining seems like a better option.

ADOPT THE ATTITUDE "WE TAKE THE FUN WITH US"

That's our mantra whenever we have a family experience. We were recently invited to a birthday party for a very small child. It was well-suited for our youngest child, but our older sons were a bit too old for the experiences. However, we reminded them of our mantra and marveled at how they intentionally created fun for themselves and other children that they met at the party. It was quite a sight to see. It's all about our perception, and it's wise for them to learn these lessons now.

Call to Action:

Seek an opportunity to make the mundane, magnificent. Stuck in traffic? Play a game of "I Spy." Long road trip? Bring along a book of knock-knock jokes or buy a CD of silly songs. Choose joy.

Daily Memories

Take Advantage of the "Small Moments."

Try to operate with the mindset that the every-day moments will make up the bulk of their childhood memories. Yes, the vacations and special occasions are memorable, but it's often the thoughts of thumb-wrestling and seat belt races that we get a chance to experience each and every day… those are the memories that we can create to make an awesome childhood experience.

Record as Much as You Can

Pictures. Videos. Journaling. Try to capture as much of this parenting journey as you can. Reviewing the memories later bring so much joy and gratitude.

The Best Advice We've Ever Received Was to "Stay Present"

This advice is so priceless, we've practiced it since becoming parents. Try not to rush towards any milestones… "I can't wait until they start walking" or "I'm looking forward to them starting school." Really try to stay present and fully experience all of it. Even the hard stuff. There is joy in all of it. There are lessons in all of it. By fully experiencing each moment, you're less likely to look back and yearn for times past. May you find the beauty in every moment and the joy in each season of your parenting. It goes by so fast.

Call to Action:

Practice being fully present in the moment. During your next crazy, hectic, overwhelming moment, take a deep breath, and fully take in your experience. What do you see? Hear? Remember that it won't always be like this.

ACKNOWLEDGMENTS

BERNETTA GRAHAM – Mommy, thank you for your sacrifice and for always doing your best. As adults, we continue to learn from your example of growth and transformation. We love you.

TED & SARAH HOUSTON – Mom & Dad, your commitment to God and example of service have blazed a trail for us. Thank you for creating an inheritance of love and faith that will bless generations to come. We love you.

DONALD MARKS – Your testimony shows us that it's never too late. "And though your beginning was small, your latter days will be very great." –Job 8:7. We love you.

RONALD GRAHAM – We celebrate the impact that you've had on our lives. Thank you for your love. We love you.

BERNETTA MARKS – Thank you for trusting us to love your babies before we realized we could. We love you.

ISHA COGBORN – Thank you for planting seeds and encouraging me to dream. The best is still yet to come. We love you.

DR. CHANTA HAYWOOD – I've admired you for so long, and I am so honored to call you mentor and friend. Thank you for your example. We love you.

PASTOR WALTER AUGUST – God really used you to pour into our lives and our marriage. We're so grateful for you and will continue to pay it forward. We love you.

PAULA WHITFIELD - Thank you for helping us get over this finish line. Your support and encouragement have blessed us more than you can imagine.

We acknowledge the many couples that have shared time with us during various seasons of our journey and celebrate those that will do so in the future. We take lessons and blessings from each connection and pray that we leave a measure of light and love along the way. Blessings to you all.

TDR & TEAM – Thank you for pushing us beyond our comfort and encouraging us to use our gifts to inspire and empower others. May you continue to reap a harvest of blessings as you honor God by living out your purpose and encouraging others to do so as well.

§

www.ingramcontent.com/pod-product-compliance
Lightning Source LLC
Chambersburg PA
CBHW071643090426
42738CB00027B/2591